Praise for *Stark Truths: Living on High Alert*

"A heart-breaking history of how it used to be - and sadly still is in many places - for a woman who loves another. *Stark Truths* is a vivid reminder that the freedoms and rights lesbians enjoy today were earned with the blood, bones, and sometimes lives of the women who came before us."

Baxter Clare Trautman, author of the L.A. Franco mystery series.

"These linked pieces of profound truth-telling span the pre-Stonewall days through the hippie era in England and the United States. Although they explore historic elements in lesbian culture, when butch and femme roles were a norm, for ex., they are also sadly current. We may have made gay marriage the law of the land, but our president just tweeted that transgendered individuals are no longer welcome in the military. Gillian Herbert's words compel us to never forget that acts of violence spring from homophobia, and that many gay people are still living closeted and traumatized as a result of these abominations. In 2016, at Pulse, the gay club in Orlando, forty-nine men, mostly Latino, were killed. Gillian is a survivor who has given those of us who have experienced anti-Semitism, xenophobia, misogyny, racism, and discrimination because we are of size, a road map to self-love and liberation."

Willa Schneberg, winner of the Oregon Book Award in Poetry, author of *Rending the Garment;* psychotherapist in private practice.

"This painful memoir about growing up lesbian in the 50's and 60's is moving testimony to the author's courage and endurance. Her stories remind me of the brave butch women who helped me come out in my youth. How grateful I am to Gillian Herbert and her generation of queers for paving the way."

Jeff Mann, author of *Cub and Country.*

"Gillian Herbert has written a heartfelt memoir about being a lesbian during a time of fear and discrimination, and her struggle to live a life outside societal norms."

Paul Alan Fahey, editor of *Equality: What Do You Think About When You Think of Equality?* and the Rainbow Award winning *The Other Man: 21 Writers Speak Candidly About Sex, Love, Infidelity, & Moving On.*

"*STARK TRUTHS* is well-named, as it is starkly painful at times, yet always truthful. Not to mention beautifully written. An important memoir."

Dennis Palumbo, psychotherapist and author.

"Exquisitely honest stories chained together with strength, courage and an unrelenting yearning for acceptance."

Eldonna Edwards, author of memoir *Lost In Transplantation* and forth coming novel *This I Know.*

"This personal, very poignant memoir is told through episodes both heartening and harrowing. The life story is woven through LGBT history, making it especially vivid, and shows us a whole stratum of human sexuality that was cruelly treated, through both hostility and incomprehension. Despite this serious setting, the author's style is engaging, the narration immediately sympathetic. An amazing range of human emotions are showcased in this individual's story."

Clare London, author of the *True Colors,
With A Kick* and *London Lads* series.

Stark Truths

Living on High Alert

Gillian P. Herbert

Copyright © 2017 by Gillian P. Herbert

All rights reserved. No part of this publication may be reproduced or transmitted in any form or by any means, electronic or mechanical, including photocopy, recording, or any information storage and retrieval system, without permission in writing from the publisher.

Requests for permission to make copies of any part of this work should be submitted online at
GPHWriter@gmail.com
Published in the United States by Gillian P. Herbert, 2017.

Twin Beds and *Ladies* were published by *Sinister Wisdom 106*.
Warning Bell, A Loud Voice, No Way Out, Open Invitation,
and *Challenging a Cop* were published simultaneously in
CALYX Journal, Vol. 30, issue 2.

Gillian is grateful to the judges of the Mendocino Coast
Writers Conference for awarding
Brownie Bravado, Fireworks, and *What's In A Word*
1st place in creative non-fiction at their 2013 conference.
Also, *Writing It Real* for selecting
Anything to Declare, Pervert, Go Dance and *Sanctuary* as
winners in their 2015 competition.

Credits:
Author Photograph: Joan Bobkoff
Cover Design: Melody W. Young
Interior Design: Melody W. Young

ISBN-978-0-9890682-9-1

*For Rita.
You have given me,
and continue to give me, your best.
I am profoundly grateful for you.
You are my love.*

"...being treated unequally really scars your soul..."

Mary Bonauto
The Rachel Maddow Show, 3/27/2013

Mary L. Bonauto is an attorney who for over twenty-five years has fought to eradicate discrimination based on sexual orientation and gender identity. She has served as the Civil Rights Project Director at GLAD since 1990. In 2015 she successfully argued before the U.S. Supreme Court in the historic case Obergefell v. Hodges, establishing the freedom to marry for same-sex couples nationwide.

Contents

Back View	15
Brownie Bravado	17
Fireworks	23
What's in a Word?	29
Letters	33
The Loudest Whisper	41
Twin Beds	47
André	53
Peace	57
Ladies	61
Anything to Declare?	69
Sanctuary	73
Pervert	77
Go Dance	81
Warning Bell	87
Open Invitation	93
No Way Out	99
A Loud Voice	105
Fair Game	107
Challenging a Cop	111
Call to Action	113
Appreciation	115
About the author	117

Back View

Sonora
California USA
2016

I pushed open the swinging door and stepped into the lobby of the restaurant. I was a few minutes late for my lunch date and glad to see my friend waiting for me. Our outstretched arms folded into a warm embrace. We had not seen each other for several years so it was a prolonged hug.

An elderly couple sat nearby. He said, "You're the second man she's greeted like that today. You'd better be careful."

My mind whirled and then I understood. He saw my blue jeans, my black jacket and my short, spiky hair, and concluded that I was a man. How to respond? Do I turn and confront him, embarrass him and his wife? Do I tell her, "Your husband is really confused!" Or do I challenge him with, "What the hell's your problem?"

We held the hug a few more seconds, and then I stepped back and looked into Heather's eyes. I told her how great she looked, keeping my back to the man. I didn't move. I held that pose until the hostess rescued us.

As we took our seats, I made a point not to look around or make eye contact with him. I acknowledged myself for not having made a fool of him, and for not making a scene, as I had no desire to do either – but I felt accosted and insulted once again.

Throughout my life, I've had to refine the art of keeping the peace, hiding and protecting myself... and others.

Brownie Bravado

Bromley, Kent
England
1951

My childhood in Bromley, south of London, was orderly and predictable. However, Thursday evenings were always exciting because it was when my Brownie pack met. Away from my parents, this junior level of the Girl Guides was where I was free to make new friends, all of us decked out in our brown dresses, yellow neck ties, brown berets and shoes. We got to run, laugh and sing, as well as work towards our craft and sports badges. At the age of eight, this felt like being a big girl who was getting her first taste of freedom.

This was my special time, when I was one of the crowd, and not the daughter of two teachers. I was still somewhat of an outsider—we had lived in Egypt for the last three years—so I was getting to know the other girls, focusing on learning their games and understanding their jokes. As the weeks passed I felt as though I was settling in and enjoying more of their activities.

Linda and I lived close to each other, so we would meet up and collect other girls on our way up

New Leamington Street to Burnt Ash Hill, skipping along the pavement to the church hall where our meetings were held.

The evenings were filled with laughter and a camaraderie that I loved. We all played hard, danced hand-in-hand in our little 'Six', sang out loud and clear, and repeated our promise to do our best:

> To love my God,
> To serve the Queen and my country,
> To help other people and
> To keep the Brownie Guide Law.

With enthusiasm our little voices chimed out the Brownie Guide Law,

A Brownie Guide thinks of others before herself and does a Good Turn every day.

The Pack was led by Brown Owl, a long suffering woman who understood that her role was to give us a good time, and find ways for us to let off steam, while laying the foundation for those of us migrating up to the Girl Guides. At the end of each meeting, Brown Owl saw us off with a loud Hoot! and a reminder to walk home together for safety.

We often ignored her warning and took the short cut across a stretch of common land, to get home faster. Muddy pathways zigzagged between scrawny bushes and trees and there was scrub grass filling the areas in between. Crossing the common was forbidden: unlit and sparsely travelled it was considered unsafe for us eight year olds. But we did it anyway.

On this particular evening we scrambled through the bushes and all seemed fine. That is, until a few of the girls started to taunt me.

"You're such a tomboy," said one of them. Her friend jumped in with "And you're always wearing your brother's shirts and shorts to play." I wanted to dispute this, but it was true. My mother saved the clothes my brother had outgrown and I wore them for play. I never minded, because it meant I could climb trees and play hard outside and never be in trouble for getting dirty.

"So what?" I yelled back.

One of them swung around, the sneer on her face catching me by surprise. Why were my friends turning on me?

"Bet you're not really a girl." said another. "Look at you! A page boy haircut and your brother's sandals."

I stopped and looked down at my feet, at my brother's shoes. I looked up and found everyone standing around me. What did they want? Was I supposed to yell...or cry?

"I am too a girl!" I spat out through tears.

"Prove it then!" someone shouted.

I stepped back, lifted my dress and dragged down my panties. "There!" I cried out in defiance.

I watched their faces pale and they looked a little scared. The air hung still for some time. As if aware a line had been crossed, they backed away, turned and ran. I adjusted my clothing and ran after them. No matter how hurt and angry I was, I didn't want to be left alone in that isolated place.

As we scattered to our homes, they sang out their goodbyes to one another and I heard latches clicking as gates closed.

I walked up our garden path, around to the back of the house, through the door and into the kitchen. Mother was cleaning the work counter and laying the table for next morning's breakfast. I ran past her, up the stairs and into my bedroom. When my father came to say good-night, I said nothing. In fact, I never told anyone of my pain, or the agonising confusion I experienced that night, when girls I thought my friends made me prove I wasn't a boy.

Fireworks

Lyme Regis, Dorset
England
1961

"Hullo," called out the girl, abandoning her luggage at the door.

"Hullo," I answered, refusing to turn my head as she entered the room. At seventeen I felt too grown up to be on holiday with my parents. And especially at a hotel that offered a special price if older teenagers—friends or complete strangers—shared a room.

This room had four single beds, each with a bedside cabinet and chest of drawers at the foot. The only saving grace was the bay window seat, where I was lounging. The back light drew a line around me—one leg straight out, one bent up—as I leaned back against the window frame.

The girl walked across the room and stood near the window seat. "Beautiful gardens," she said. I nodded.

She turned to me, "I'm Jean."

I lifted my eyes from the garden flower beds and said, "I'm Gill."

She stood there, legs slightly apart, hands

thrust into the pockets of her drainpipe trousers, and did a little bounce on to her toes. She smiled. "Have you explored the place yet?" When I shook my head, she gestured towards the door. "Come on, let's see the rest of this place."

Reluctantly, I unwound myself, dropped my feet to the floor and stood up. I wasn't very interested, but boredom pushed me to follow Jean out the door and down the corridor.

We wandered through the games room, past table tennis tables, and through the dining room, which was set for dinner with white linen and plates. We passed the library and the tennis courts and ended up at the pool. We chattered on. "Where are you from?" "Who did you come with?" "What do you do?" "How old are you?" "Do you have brothers or sisters?" I learnt Jean came from Birmingham, was an only child and taught games and physical exercise in an elementary school.

"Here's our first secret," she said, laughing. "My parents knocked three years off my age so I could share a room!"

I told about myself, my older brother—who wasn't on this trip—and my school teacher parents who'd dragged me to this hotel. At the time, I was in my last year in a hotel and restaurant training programme.

Standing with our backs to the pool, we could see terraced gardens on the hillside below. Beds of roses climbed over arbours along the winding pathways. We ambled through the garden and curled up on opposite ends of a bench. Our conversation was a bit reserved at first with Jean doing all the work, but slowly I began to loosen up and eventually we laughed. I remember leaning back, relaxing as I enjoyed her warmth and openness

Our chat was broken by a clanging bell, announcing afternoon tea. We returned to the main house and parted as we joined our families. Later, our paths crossed as we retreated to our room to dress for dinner, but time was short and we barely spoke.

A social event in the main recreational hall followed the evening meal. There was a small group of musicians and an emcee who called the dances. It started out with country square dancing, where adults, teens and children all mingled, with much laughter and missteps.

It was around nine-thirty when the musicians took a refreshment break. The smaller children were whisked off to bed, while more adults, drinks in hand, drifted in from the bar. The noise level dropped and quiet murmured conversation swirled about.

When the musicians returned, they played softer, quieter music fit for ballroom dancing. Couples of all ages took to the floor, including some of the older, more genteel guests. Within minutes, the range of dancers gliding elegantly across the room ran from young adults to silver-haired couples.

Several times that night I danced with my father. As a child, I'd learnt to dance by standing on his shoes and being whirled around our living room. In my early teenage years I was expected to stand on my own feet, so he'd taught me the steps to basic ballroom dances. But most of the evening he swept by with my mother in his arms. They cut a dashing couple, moving well and talking quietly to each other.

Two women danced by our table. A quick glance around the room made it clear that there was a shortage of men. This was 1961, and Britain was still struggling under the enormous loss of life in WWII. Over three hundred and eighty thousand men were killed, resulting in a dramatic scarcity of men between the ages of thirty-five and fifty.

A quiet voice drew my attention back to our table. Jean had slipped into the chair next to me. "Gill," she said. "I saw you dancing with your father. Would you dance with me?"

We edged on to the floor and were soon drawn into the circling throng. I got used to her arms around me, her body guiding me with a gentle touch. She danced well so I relaxed and enjoyed myself. We danced several times that evening and I was struck by the ease I felt with her. My gangly teenage awkwardness seemed to drop away and I found myself laughing easily. I was delighted to be there, and surprised at myself for feeling this way.

When the event broke up, I kissed my parents goodnight and promised to be down for breakfast at eight-thirty. We went our separate ways, my folk heading upstairs to their bedroom, while I rushed back to my room where I grabbed my sponge bag and dashed to the bathroom. I'd never shared a bedroom and I wanted to be in my pyjamas, in bed, while still alone.

Maybe I dozed. A few, small noises from outside the room drifted by on the edge of my consciousness, and I enjoyed the warmth, as I hunkered down in my blankets. When the room light went out, I relaxed even more and let my mind wander over the day, full and interesting, wondering what tomorrow would bring. Would Jean and I spend more time together? Would we swim or play table-tennis? Would she hold me gently as we danced again? I smiled as I delicately explored these possibilities.

A hand shook my shoulder, causing me to start. Opening my eyes I saw Jean and heard her say, "Gill, it's okay. It's just me, Jean."

I sank back on my pillow.

"Gill, I'm really cold. Can I come in with you and get warm?"

I pulled back the bedding and she slipped in next to me, sliding her arms across my chest and her head rested next to mine. I turned onto my side, my back to her. We lay spooned together, chatting quietly, my body quickly adjusting to her softness and warmth. Jean's hands gently stroked my shoulders and she ran her fingers through my hair. Her touch was comforting.

After a few minutes, I squirmed out of her arms and, with much giggling as I tried not to fall off the narrow bed, managed to turn over. Now, facing each other, I stroked her face and hair, and she kissed me. It was a soft, tender kiss, and I returned it as I felt her body breathing into mine. Our kisses grew deeper as our hands explored our bodies. I'd never done this before, never been in a situation where it could be done. It felt so right, so natural. Her hands drifted over my entire body until I knew nothing other than the sensation of pleasure. I was on fire and Jean moved quickly and decisively to release the fireworks.

I turned my head into her shoulder and lay still—but still vibrating. We were silent. I felt safe in her arms. We drifted off to sleep.

Hours later I felt Jean shift and I opened my eyes. The sky was lightening as dawn approached. She slipped out of my bed and into hers. "Go back to sleep," she said.

"And Gill," she added, "You can't tell anyone about this. You hear me?"

I nodded, closed my eyes and snuggled down. I was cold. I didn't understand why, but I knew this was our secret.

What's in a Word?

Eltham, London
England
1961

Our local library was a tall, dark building, with huge pillars, silent and pale, standing on either side of the entry stairs. Years of scurrying feet had worn dips in those concrete steps. I remember clutching piles of books and following other readers into the brightly lit general lending area, where a librarian sat at the central carousel as she took in returned books and checked dates for overdue fees. A second librarian stamped due dates in those books being taken out. The stamp made a loud, metallic clacking noise every time she banged it down on a book. Clackity-clackity-clack. The rules of the library were clearly displayed: three books per reader, whispers only. With imposing stacks of books all around me, and the high windows at the top of the walls, the library felt solemn and purposeful.

It was the first Saturday after our return from holiday, and I needed answers. I avoided the main room, and entered through the swinging glass doors of the Reference Library. This room was a sharp contrast to the main library: it was even quieter, a kind of inner sanctum, for those who took their research seriously

A librarian sat behind a small desk. Next to her was a large catalogue file that stretched the length of the room. She looked up at with me with surprise. Clearly she thought I was in the wrong place. I ignored her and walked back along the row of files. I needed to do this on my own.

But how? I didn't know the right word, so I started with a word I did know: Homosexual. I knew that this was what they called men who loved other men. I opened the "H" drawer, all the time keeping a covert eye on the librarian. Whenever I caught her glance, I focused on the file cards. No, said my concentration, I do not need any help, thank you.

Eventually I had scribbled enough reference numbers. I walked through the stacks, gathered several books and retreated to a desk back in a corner. I switched on the brass desk lamp and slid onto the chair. I recall how very alone I felt sitting in the bright circle of light. The darkness surrounding me came from the dimly lit room, and my own sense of isolation.

As the hours passed, I felt bolder and ventured out for a few more books. Soon I had the word that had been escaping me: Lesbian. I was a lesbian. The fingers of my left hand caressed the deep grain of the oak desk: the wood felt warm and smooth between the sharp ridges. The fingers of my right hand played with the corners of the book pages, repeatedly riffling them. I read quietly for over an hour.

Isolated in my corner, I began to understand that everything I read was bad news. I didn't believe I was 'deviant' or 'perverted' or 'psychologically immature', but I did understand now why Jean had been so emphatic with her "tell no-one." Clearly she'd known lesbianism was unacceptable, how wrong it was, and how we needed to hide.

Leaning back in my chair, I gazed through one of the high windows at the grey sky with dark, looming clouds threatening rain. My mind took me back to Jean, how she laughed as she beat me at table tennis, our yells as we swam in the freezing pool. I could hear our voices sharing stories as we took long walks, and feel those nights we shared, filled with warmth and tenderness.

I re-shelved all the books, making sure they were in line with the rest. Walking home, I kicked at the gravel stones as I struggled to reconcile the joy I'd experienced with the bleakness of the damning judgements I'd read. I knew that my life had changed; I just didn't know how much.

Letters

Eltham, London
England
1961

Each afternoon I checked the post to see if another thick and stubby envelope had arrived, postmarked Weston-Super-Mare, Somerset. If I was lucky, I'd take it and rush to my room. Jean had warned me often not to save her letters, to throw them away in case my parents found them. A letter from a friend was one thing, but Jean's letters were different. But I kept them, hidden in one of Dad's discarded cigar boxes that I tucked away in the bottom drawer of my dressing table.

Safe in my bedroom, I'd unfold the many pages with Jean's small regular handwriting, hungry for every word. She told about the classes she was teaching and her students, with added tales about the school's staff, and their after-school gatherings at the local pub. I read about those long, quiet weekends when she slept late and then read student papers. About the tennis and netball matches she coached. And how much she missed me. When was I coming to visit? she always asked.

By late September I'd saved enough from my

first job as a Catering Officer in a local hospital to buy train tickets. Letters flew between us—letters of excitement as we scanned train timetables. The plan was for me to get the train to Charing Cross Station on Friday morning, then the tube to Paddington Station, and the main line train to the West Country. If I caught the 1:30 train I'd arrive in Somerset in the late afternoon. My return journey would be on Monday. Two whole days—three nights—no one else—no obligations—just us.

The week before my departure passed so slowly. Every day I tried hard to distract myself, afraid I'd reveal my excitement about seeing this woman I loved. I spent time clearing out cupboards in my bedroom, my form of spring cleaning, but it was still a challenge to keep my hands busy and my mouth shut.

My big dilemma was what to pack. I only had two pairs of trousers. Mother couldn't understand the fuss; a pleated skirt would look nice, she insisted, so what was my problem? My problem was I felt like a frilly cupcake in it, and I knew that Mother knew that. From childhood I'd always preferred shorts and trousers, but my mother bought my clothes and her view was pretty conventional. I settled on wearing one pair of trousers, and packing the other along with several blouses, sports shirts, and a jacket. It would have to be enough.

Friday finally arrived, and Dad dropped

me off at the station where I caught the train to Charing Cross, ran down the outside tiled steps to the Underground, and leapt on the Circle line to Paddington. So far this was all familiar since I'd taken this route to college. I was in new territory at Paddington Station and felt anxious as to whether I'd catch the right train. As I stood in the queue to buy my return trip ticket, I wondered if Jean would still love me with such passion and tenderness. I now understood more clearly the forbidden world I'd entered, so felt fearful as to whether our love would still hold true.

Stations flew by as we rattled across England. From my window seat I gazed out on the passing countryside, but I saw nothing. I was oblivious to ticket inspectors, to passengers getting on and off the train: I was floating in my private world.

When I stepped off the train, I glanced down the platform and through the ticket gate. Would she remember I was coming? What if she forgot... or didn't care? And then I saw her, standing outside the ticket barrier, so nonchalant, one hand in her pocket, the other slightly raised. She wore a broad grin and I ran to her. We hugged and laughed, and then rushed out of the station and caught a bus to her basement flat. I registered nothing during the ride except the firm hand holding mine and the thrill of anticipation that surrounded us.

The flat was warm and cosy, and being slightly

below ground level made it feel more like a cocoon. Doors and walls kept out the world. The days flew by; we shared breakfast in bed and ate our other meals curled up together on the couch. We took walks on the pier and along the seafront and lay in deck chairs sunning ourselves. In the evening, we cuddled in front of the television and watched old films. The rabbit ears made for a poor antenna, but we still watched, unfazed by the fuzzy picture. Our nights were warm and rich, cuddling and giggling, kissing, exploring and enjoying. We were together; nothing else mattered.

Monday arrived too quickly. On the train heading home, I felt every mile that separated us. At times I stared at the floor of the train, avoiding the exchange of glances with other passengers. How could I reconcile the beauty of our passion with the damnation I'd read in the reference library? This contradiction tore at me. I knew we were not perverted, no matter what I read. I just knew it. But I had no idea how my parents, or my brother, would react. I'd never heard them talk about homosexuality or lesbianism. But I wasn't brave enough to speak out.

A busy work schedule distracted me from my loneliness. I laughed as my co-workers told their home and heart stories, but I knew to keep mine to myself. On weekends I hung out with Ian, my closest friend from college. We'd been part of a small class, five girls and six boys, all bright, but not academic. Learning the hotel and restaurant trade together, our goal had been to work in high-end hotels. I'd found the boys hard working, but rough and arrogant. Except, that is, for Ian. With his starched collars, neatly knotted ties, freshly pressed suit, shiny shoes, and hair always neatly combed, he was perfect. Perfectly turned out, perfect attendance and, invariably, perfect homework. What wasn't so great was how his perfection had brought relentless teasing from the other boys. Our friendship worked for us both; we accepted each other in a way others did not.

I enjoyed Ian's smile and his old-fashioned courtesy. He opened doors, carried my books and lifted heavy equipment in the kitchen for me. I was the most awkward of the girls. Attending an all girl's high school had given me no experience with boys. In addition, my mother had never known how to dress me, so there was nothing stylish or feminine about me. But Ian and I hung out together and we laughed. In our two years at college, we held hands, kissed occasionally and attended the college dances together. On the train to college every day I listened to his odd comments about how the other boys bullied him.

Many years later I learnt that Ian was gay. Unable to handle the rejection and pressure, he committed suicide. Today, so many decades later, I still wonder, would his life have been different, more bearable, if I'd had the courage to speak my truth?

In December I boarded another train that carried me to Jean. This time we huddled under an umbrella in the rain, and took walks along the sea front as crashing waves pounded over the seawall. Foul weather kept the paths empty, so we were alone, which created a sense of safety. Nevertheless, our real safety was felt inside Jean's flat, our entertainment, beyond the fuzzy TV, was the two of us alone.

For the first time in my life I experienced how it felt to be enough, just as I was. No longer the odd child, but now the much-loved woman.

When I returned home, aglow with Jean's warmth and love, Christmas festivities filled my days. I entered into the spirit with enthusiasm even though I knew not to talk of my joy. I felt strong now, complete. I propped up Jean's Christmas card in my room and smiled at it.

The week between Christmas and New Year brought no letter. I was disappointed but understood that the post was often delayed at this time of year. By the second week in January I became worried and wondered at the silence. When the familiar envelope finally arrived, I carried it to my room. Holding it, I wondered why it was so thin. I hesitated before ripping it open. I held my breath as I scanned the words: Jean loved me dearly, but we could not continue to meet. There was no future for us. She wanted to marry, to have children, to progress in her teaching career without fear.

I sat on the side of my bed working to control a heartbreak I knew I would have to hide from everyone. No public tears, no public grief, no solace. I folded her letter and buried it in the box. When my mother called me to supper I started down the stairs slowly. My feet landed heavily on each tread, echoing the hopelessness felt by my battered heart.

The Loudest Whisper

London
England
1962

When I graduated from the hotel and restaurant college, I was told to spend the next two years working in a range of different facilities. The idea was to move around, get experience and find a good fit for my talents.

I took this advice seriously. In 1962, after working six months in a hospital's catering unit, I applied to the Regent Palace Hotel. It sat on Piccadilly Circus, in the heart of London. I was offered a position as Floor Food Manager, which required that I be on call twenty-four hours a day. With proximity an issue, I was required to live in the staff building.

I was eighteen and this was my first adventure at living away from home. I was excited by the opportunity to explore London, take advantage of free art shows, music concerts and cheap, standing-room-only theatre tickets...all at places that were just around the corner. Despite London being a bustling and colourful city, I was painfully aware that I was without family or friends, and carried in my heart an essential aloneness I'd come to understand that previous summer in the reference library.

I enjoyed my work, but when those around me gossiped about their dates or their latest love, I smiled and kept my secret. I felt so disconnected from everyone around me that I persuaded someone at the local parking garage to squeeze my moped into a corner so I could hop on it and ride home whenever I needed family food and hugs.

As a supervisor, I had a room of my own. I was the envy of most of the staff as they—chamber maids and food service maids—had to share rooms. Many were young girls from Ireland, and I had a hard time understanding their speech and their culture. This did not stop me from recognizing snippets of gossip or noticing glances and quick hugs that passed between some of the maids. The meaning was not lost on me when I heard shouts of delight because two young women had negotiated a room change so they could be together. But nobody spoke to me or invited me in: I was a supervisor and not part of their group. And the only other supervisor in residence was a dashingly beautiful, older woman who barely acknowledged me. It was a lonely time.

One day the gossip mill brought the news of a film, "The Loudest Whisper," which was based on Lillian Hellman's controversial play "The Children's Hour." Written in 1934, and considered by many to be scandalous and deserving of being blacklisted, it dealt with two school teachers accused of having a lesbian relationship. I was incredulous that there was a main stream film about lesbians and I wanted to see it, but I was afraid I'd lose my job if anyone saw me in the cinema. After a while, I pushed aside my inner arguments and determined to go.

I waited until mid afternoon, when I thought there was less chance of anyone from work spotting me, and sidled up to the box office to buy a ticket. I sat mid-row, mid-theatre in the almost empty place, hoping for anonymity. And then I watched in fascination as the story unfolded. Audrey Hepburn and Shirley MacLaine were the headmistresses of a private school for girls. One of those girls, bent on revenge for having been punished, swears she saw the women together, and in an intimate way. The lie spins out of control, forcing the closure of the school—what decent parent would allow a child to remain?—and culminating in a lawsuit. Ultimately, the slander is proven untrue, but the devastation has already ruined two lives.

I sat in the theatre, the credits rolling, and wondered: Was this to be my life?

Deep in thought, I was interrupted by noises behind me. The rustling of clothing and shifting in the seat. I ignored it. Then audible breathing joined the other noises. I tossed a quick glance over my shoulder and saw a man a couple of rows back, sprawled in his seat, his knees wide apart. His fly was open and he was masturbating with deep, long strokes.

I slid down in my seat as I turned away. Did I complain? No, because such a deviant and perverted topic in such an intolerant society placed this film in the category of aberrant sex, not for decent people. If I were the women on that screen, and they were damned, then who was I to damn him?

I exited quickly and pushed my way into the throngs on the street. Five minutes later, I was riding my moped, threading my way through the dense traffic, heading for home and hugs. The depth of my aloneness was profound.

Twin Beds

London
England
1962

Later that year I became the front-desk receptionist at a private and high-end residential club in central London. It offered accommodations and food services for its members, and an assortment of educational events.

My main task was to run the telephone switchboard, so old that it had little dolls' eyes that flicked up and down for each receiver. There were plug-in keys attached to cords, each one connecting the various callers. I was also expected to provide whatever assistance the residents needed, take reservations, prepare guests' bills and collect payment.

Every day I prepared a summary of the billing work. At eleven o'clock sharp I'd hear the clickety-clack of stiletto high heels on the marble staircase as the bookkeeper came down to pick up my reports and the daily take. Tall and slender, June had deep auburn hair swept back in a beehive, and wore flashy jewellery that set off her fashionable clothes. I felt like a real country bumpkin in my pleated skirts, twinset top and cardigans and casual shoes. I enjoyed my work, but the daily pickup by June always made me anxious. And not without cause, because she'd often return to explain what I'd entered incorrectly and how to make it right. I began to spend extra time on this task, hoping to avoid her repeat visits. Somehow, I failed to master the intricacies of the financial reports, but my anxiety lessened as June and I became friends. Eventually, we would laugh over a cup of coffee as she walked me through my latest miscalculations.

One day I saw a notice of an evening lecture by a famous explorer. Although these meetings were not usually open to staff, I requested and was granted permission to attend.

The next morning the clickety-clack of stiletto heels told me my teacher was on her way to give me yet another lesson. I steeled myself and was pleasantly surprised when I heard, "Gill, I just found out you're going to the lecture next week." When I asked how she knew, she told me that she had also asked for permission to attend, and that my name was mentioned. And then she asked me to join her for dinner before the event. As much as I felt out of her class, I accepted. We agreed to meet at her place for dinner. With that she turned with a swirl of her skirt and clickety-clacked her way back up the stairs.

A couple of days later, after having omitted

some subtotalling that June found useful on the report, she arrived at my desk. Once we had everything in order, she asked how I would get home after the lecture. I lived in the suburbs and assumed I'd have to leave early and hail a taxi to catch the last train. When she suggested I stay at her place, I stumbled over a response. I barely knew her, so what should I say?

"Thanks. That might be really good."

"Good. Just throw your stuff in a bag and bring it with you to work. This'll make it so much easier for you."

Come Friday evening, June collected me and my bag from the front desk and we walked along Hyde Park, round Marble Arch to Upper Berkeley Street. I followed her up the steps of a Regency style house that had been converted into many small bedsits. June's was on the ground floor, one large room with twin beds and an area for sitting adjacent to a built in kitchen. The bathroom was down the hall and shared by several renters.

June served a delicious home-made cannelloni and a full-bodied red wine. She chattered about her family, her trips to Italy and her love of cooking. I ate and smiled, but felt very awkward. She had travelled extensively and seemed so sophisticated and worldly, while my own childhood travels with my parents seemed insignificant, and I'd been nowhere since leaving college the year before. We were poles apart, but we laughed a lot.

We made it to the lecture on time, but had to stand in the back because we were staff. It didn't seem to matter because I was so busy wondering how I'd got caught up in this adventure. Why wasn't I home in my bed?

After the lecture we mingled with guests and I heard June's laughter floating over to me as she chatted and flirted in an easy, friendly style. I knew she was only two years older than I, but her self-assurance and poise overwhelmed me.

Back at her flat, she told me that we had to be quiet because her flatmate would already be in bed. She told me to use the bathroom first and then slip into the bed on the right, her bed. In the bathroom I brushed my teeth and put on my pyjamas, gazing into the mirror and thinking about this plan: that June and I were going to sleep in the same bed. I hadn't understood this and wondered if it was too late to dress and find my way home. Realizing I had no choice, I scurried down the hallway and slipped into her bed. It felt strange to curl up in someone else's bed, to be sleeping on their sheets, but I was tired and had had too much to drink.

A few minutes later June slipped in and curled around me. I feigned sleep, believing the sooner she slept, the sooner I could relax and sleep. We lay motionless for a while, but I sensed she was still awake. Why? As I asked myself this question, I felt her arm encircle me and pull me close. She gently brushed my hair from my face and murmured in my ear, "Gill, I know you're awake and waiting. I'm here now." She turned my face and kissed me deeply. My mind spun as my body responded. Clearly she had set this up, had wanted me in her bed, but we worked together and this could be disastrous. How did I get here?

Our lovemaking was fierce and passionate, much deeper and more demanding than my time with Jean. June was an experienced lover and she knew how to get what she needed. I was an eager student. We slept little.

In the morning, her roommate was gone, apparently unaware or unperturbed by our love making. June and I barely made it to work on time. As we walked she told me, her voice almost teasing, that she'd never slept with a woman before but thought it would be fun to explore. She explained how hard she'd worked to create accounting errors in my work so she could chat with me. She'd felt strongly that I would be open to her advances, although a little scared on the outside chance she was wrong.

Had I seen her carefully constructed seduction? Not one bit of it! But I was ready when yet again I was warned not to discuss this with anyone. Despite her assurance we would get sacked if our boss found out, the desperate loneliness that had formed a hard shell around me now had a crack in it.

André

London
England
1962

June and I met André on one of our forays into the city's underworld of basement cafes and bars. Seedy, dirty, usually unlicensed and often illegal establishments, they catered to those living on the edge: prostitutes, pimps, drug dealers and users, bookies and touters, transvestites, homosexuals and petty criminals. Here we could hold hands, cuddle, be recognised as lesbians...and ignored.

André sashayed over to our table and dropped into a chair. "I saw you two and thought I'd drop in for a chat." He asked if we were new to this place, and the three of us chatted. June was more talkative than I, having grown up in a rough world and acquiring an ease that I lacked. Despite this I laughed quite easily with him, and we bought him coffee. He was tall, skinny, sickly pale, with long, heavily nicotine-stained fingers. His stringy black hair dropped forward over one eye. As I got to know him, I realised that was a shield he hid behind. He wore thick pan-stick makeup, and below plucked and heavily pencilled eyebrows were eyelashes thick with clumpy mascara. The tight black jeans and black sweater added an air of decadence to his already unusual appearance.

Several more visits to the cafe and André was hanging out with us regularly. I didn't particularly like him. He was fidgety, constantly twiddling his fingers and rearranging his body into different poses as he sat. His high nervous laugh grated. And he was smarmy and sleazy, always looking for the wealthy man who could afford what he had to offer. But we knew so few who lived in this world and we so needed to feel welcomed and befriended. Gradually, as the three of us shared our stories, June and I came to trust him.

That is, until the phone rang one evening when I was home at my parents' house. I was surprised to hear his voice and asked how he knew this number. I had told him that I lived with my family, but not where. "Oh," he said, "I have my ways!" And then he asked if I could loan him £5 and bring it to the cafe on Saturday. He promised to pay it back. Reluctantly, I agreed, although £5 was half of my weekly pay, and represented a lot of money.

When I told June, she was emphatic that loaning money to André was the same as kissing it goodbye. Despite his promises, he didn't pay me back. Four weeks later he called again with the same request. I mumbled something about not being sure. That Saturday evening when he approached me, I told him I had nothing for him. His face became flushed and he swore at me as he stormed out.

The next call came two weeks later. Again, I told him I didn't have any money, but this time the game had changed. André shocked me by saying that he had checked at my local bank and my account had a balance of £55...and he was right. He quickly added that either I give him the money, or he would tell my father where I went on Saturday nights, and with whom. "I'll make it public," he threatened. He knew my father was a much-respected local school head-master and that he didn't know I was a lesbian. I trembled as I hung up.

I told June of André's threat and she was furious at him and at me. Neither of us knew what to do. We couldn't go to the police, knowing that a male prostitute blackmailing a lesbian would not interest them. They'd laugh us out the station.

We decided never to go back to the cafe, but for weeks I sweated every time I walked in the front door of my home. Had André told my parents? Would they tell me if he had? I couldn't ask. I even scoured the local newspaper for any juicy story about a head master's salacious lesbian daughter. Over time, June and I came to understand that nothing was going to happen. André's threats were empty, but my awareness of our vulnerability became deeper.

Peace

Blackheath, London
England
1963

I lowered my motorbike onto its kick stand, stood back and stared at the huge white mansion. Standing amongst green bushes and trees, and despite the gentle hum of traffic in the background, it was serene and elegant. Blackheath Common had once resembled its name, a wide and open land with many expensive homes among its fields. Now it was mostly built up, yet it still managed to have islands of affluence and calm.

I considered the house and its residents, one of whom was Rachel Pearse, the headmistress of the girl's high school I had attended for five years. Founded in 1877, it was one of London's most prestigious schools. Overseen by the Clothworkers' Company, one of London's historic guilds, it was steeped in tradition and history. As a pupil, I'd often stood in line outside Miss Pearse's door for yet one more infraction. Treating my misdemeanours with humour, she'd always let me know my deed was wrong, not I. Standing outside her house, wearing my black leather jacket, jeans and boots, I felt appalled by what I'd done.

So why was I standing at her door, filled with embarrassment and dread? A few weeks earlier June and I had broken up. She'd woken me in the middle of the night with a foot squarely in the middle of my back. Pushing me out of bed and onto the floor, she'd hissed, "If you won't live with me, you can damn well go home." I'd dragged on my clothes and left. In the following days she'd refused to answer the phone. By the next weekend I knew we were through. So there I was heartbroken and alone...again.

I did my best to get through the days...and the nights. But one particularly difficult night, despair pushed me to a bar, where I got drunk. To this day I'm not sure why I chose to call my former headmistress. Perhaps I believed Rachel would guide me through my conflict. I knew that I wasn't bad, although the world around me thought I was, but Rachel had been different. She was a woman who always found the good in me. So when she answered the phone at 2.00 a.m. and calmly told me to go to bed and sleep, and then come to her flat in the morning, I was relieved and comforted.

I awoke hung over and dismayed about calling Rachel in the middle of the night. She knew my father. What if she told him of my wild behaviour? I was shocked by my audacity and stupidity, yet I had no alternative but to show up and take my chances. Standing her up was not an option. Even though it had been several years since I had left school, I still held her in respect and awe.

The building had been divided into an upper and lower residence. Rachel lived upstairs with her sister, both women spinsters and devout Quakers. I hesitated before ringing the bell. What could I tell her, other than the truth? Alcohol, broken-hearted, lesbian: all bad news.

Rachel opened the door, her soft smile and warm hug the welcome I needed. We walked along the high-ceilinged hallway of deep carpet to a warm and sunny room. The chairs and couches looked comfortable, their subtle grey-striped fabric inviting. On a small table stood a tray with a coffee pot, cups and saucers and a plate of Garibaldi biscuits. We sat across from each other and she poured us coffee, at the same time asking about my parents and my work. Once settled, she sat back in her chair. "Gill," she said, "tell me what this is all about."

I told her. She listened quietly. She topped up my coffee as she asked a few questions. I filled in the missing pieces. Finally, she looked at me and said, "Oh Gill, what a pickle you're in!"

Understatement of the year, I thought.

The quiet enfolded us as we sat together, pupil and mentor, and I imagined her sorting through her years of experience with young women. What would she tell me? I'd already learnt that high school crushes on older girls were frequent, with furtive meetings on quiet corridors and stair wells, those glancing smiles at morning assembly, passion expressed in letters slipped from small hand to small hand or hidden in desks. All of this existed, but was forbidden. On my part, I had experienced those deeply passionate attachments and adorations, but never any physical contact beyond the occasional hug. Rachel had known this about me, but had never criticized.

"And I don't think alcohol has helped!" she suddenly added. "Do you have any thoughts on where you might go from here?" Her gentle voice cut through my wandering memories and pulled me back.

"None," I replied.

There was another lengthy silence—I remember thinking that she might be praying for me—and then she told me that I was so bright, and an adventurer. I waited for the "But...". Instead, she suggested that I seek a complete change, perhaps find a new direction for my life. Her solution was a stint in Voluntary Service Overseas, an international anti-poverty organisation. She offered to send me information and write a letter in support of my application.

We hugged warmly as she walked me back to the front door. I clattered down the front steps thinking that I didn't want a new direction. What I wanted was for her to step into my confusion and help me find some peace!

Ladies

London
England
1963

June and I were able to reach a compromise: I lived at home but stayed with her on weekends. Every Friday evening I'd take the train back to my home in the suburbs, climb onto my motorcycle and ride to her bedsit. At the same time, June was preparing dinner, having picked up groceries on her way home. Our timing was impeccable; she was serving dinner just as I was dropping the bike onto its kick stand and running up the stairs.

Most Saturdays were pretty mundane. We slept late and did the laundry, followed by an afternoon at the cinema and then dinner before late night clubbing. Sundays were even lazier, with newspapers and coffee in a nearby cafe.

Until the day I got her phone call telling me that there was a tiny one-roomed flat around the corner from her place, and that I needed to see it at once, before it was rented.

What I found was an empty space, bare walls, naked light bulb and an unfinished wooden floor. There was a small kitchen, more like a walled-off corridor with a sink, and the bathroom was shared with the unit on the floor below. Dust and cobwebs were everywhere, but it was on the top floor with lots of light from the two windows overlooking the street. The narrow, Edwardian building was set in the middle of a small terrace. It had an antique shop on the ground floor, with a side door that led to stairs up to the two flats.

I knew we could make this comfortable. I would paint the walls and floor and put up rails for the curtains June would sew. Shelving in a corner would hold our books, and we'd round up old furniture from relatives and paint it. We could make this a safe haven right in the heart of the West End.

The next Saturday we were up early for a trip to John Lewis, a department store on Oxford Street. Established back in 1864 as a haberdashery and rebuilt after heavy wartime bombing, it carried a wonderful assortment of furnishing fabrics. With paint swatches in hand, we set out to find the right fabric for curtains.

Row after row of materials filled the wall shelves and racks. Strong colours shouted out as they nestled alongside more subdued tones. Sales clerks slid up and down behind the counters pulling out bolts of fabric as they followed customers' pointing fingers.

I stood quietly, a little bewildered, as I watched the movement of colour and heard fabric described by texture, weight and fibre. June jumped right in and marched among the displays, considering and rejecting, until yanking out a roll and nodding decisively. Clearly, this was the right one.

I left her queuing at the cashier's window while I followed the signs to the Ladies. Finally, the arrows led to a door on a landing just aside the staircase. I pushed open the door, crossed the black and white tiled floor past a couple of women washing their hands, stepped into a stall and shot the bolt. As I unbuttoned my jeans I heard a woman say in low voice, "Did you see that?" After a moment she added, "A man just went into that stall. Didn't you see him?" Her voice seemed to rise an octave as she squawked with indignation.

I looked down at my blue jeans and knee-high black leather riding boots, at my black leather jacket and the crash helmet on the floor. I started to shake and knew I was in trouble. I sat very still, as if silence would hide me.

"You stay here; I'm going to get my husband! Don't let him get out. My husband will give him what for. How dare he come in here?"

The door slammed as she ran for help, leaving me scared witless. This was 1963. Exposure as a woman in men's clothing would trigger not only righteous indignation but possibly physical abuse. I could get roughed up if her husband believed I was a man. I knew I couldn't be arrested for cross-dressing—I was wearing at least one item of women's clothing—but I could be arrested for disturbing the peace.

When more women came into the bathroom, the tale was retold, the others warned about the man in the stall. I barely listened to the indignant protests from each new arrival; I was too busy struggling to hold down my panic and trying to decide what to do. I considered climbing over the partition and into the next stall, but what if I landed on some unsuspecting woman? I considered going out the window, but we were two floors up. I decided brazenness was the better part of stupidity so I buttoned my jeans, zipped up my jacket and strapped on my crash helmet. I squared my shoulders, grabbed the bolt latch and took a deep breath.

With a quick flip of the bolt, I was out and half way to the door before the women realised I was on the move. Throwing a gruff "Sorry" at them, I charged the door with one shoulder. As it swung back, it caught a man outside and flung him back against the wall. I took two strides and leapt down the stairs, the woman behind me shrieking, "That's him! Get him!"

Feet thundered above my head as I ran. I didn't look up or around. I just ran. Suddenly the doors to the street were ahead so I crashed them open and ran for my bike. I leapt onto it, turned the key and dropped it into first gear. For the first ten yards of my escape, there was a man running alongside, grabbing at the bike, yelling, "You slimy bastard. Scaring my wife. Just let me get my hands on you." I didn't give him a chance. I picked up speed and left his voice trailing after me, "Bloody good beating is what I'll give you."

Free of him, I circled back and saw June standing on the kerb. Tapping the horn, I pulled in and scooped her up. As we took off, she screamed in my ear, "Why did you leave me? How dare you?"

I couldn't speak and she had no way to see my tears. As soon as I could, I pulled over and told her what had happened. She held me close as I shook. "You idiot," she said, railing at me. "Why did you go in the Ladies?"

"I needed to pee," I said softly.

She wanted to go back and confront them, her face angry, her eyes flashing. "Enough for today," I said, "We've got our curtains. Let's go home."

Anything to Declare?

Gatwick, Kent
England
1963

June and I giggled and wiggled as we strapped ourselves into the narrow plane seats. The plane was small and rickety, but we didn't notice, we were on our way to Amsterdam! Holland was known for having a history of tolerance toward homosexuality, much more so than England where, in 1963, being a lesbian was considered totally deplorable. Most of the time we felt forced to hide our relationship from friends, family, co-workers and strangers. Our only safe place was in our flat, and even then the landlord had the right to evict us. No matter where we went, lesbians were not only unwelcome, but often reviled.

Oh, but Amsterdam was different! We were so excited to explore this city where we could dance together, dine out together and even book a room with a double bed without causing a scandal. We were growing tired of our social life in London, which was restricted to seedy cafes and basement bars frequented by prostitutes, drug addicts and transvestites. For our male friends, their sexual behaviour was illegal: for us, we were just unsavoury and undesirable. Police raids often caught us, as lesbians, in their sweep. In Holland we found gracefully appointed bars with elegant dance floors, venues where membership was exclusively gay and lesbian. It was with some trepidation that we dressed for our evening out. Would we get in? Could we afford it? We dressed in our best and ordered a taxi. We whispered our destination to the driver, who then brayed it back loudly enough for the entire hotel lobby to hear. I cringed. I didn't yet understand I had nothing to fear.

The staff greeted us warmly, offering us a free guest membership as our coats were carried off to the cloakroom. We were escorted onto the main dance floor area and seated at a floor-side table. A cute gay waiter served us complimentary drinks and welcomed us. June and I watched men dance, and occasionally a couple of women floated by, all the time exchanging glances with each other. Was this really as safe as it looked? Taking a chance, we swung onto the floor, cutting through the dancers with ease. An award-winning ballroom dancer, June sparkled as she moved, while I'd learnt to lead well. Together, for the first time ever, we could pivot, glide and turn with ease and grace. We flew.

The days spun by in a blur of evenings dining out, nights of dancing and laughter and long, lazy mornings in bed. Afternoon forays into the winding cobbled streets and out onto the canals for boat rides delighted us. But perhaps our greatest excitement came from being ignored. No one stared or sneered when we held hands. No one swore or pushed us around. We were just two more women on holiday.

One day, while out walking, we rounded a corner and came upon a bookstore selling English-language books. And not just any books, but paperbacks imported from the States: lesbian pulp fiction, tales of women living like us in the shadows. Books with titles like Odd Girl Out by Ann Bannon, and Stranger on Lesbos by Valerie Taylor. The covers were garish and loud, the stories heartbreaking, but we found ourselves—our fears and dreams...and lives—in their pages. Every day we picked up a few more books and spent rainy afternoons curled up on our bed as we devoured them.

On our last day in Amsterdam we surveyed the stack of books as we packed our suitcases. These were books banned in the UK, books we could go to jail for possessing, considered contraband if we dared to take them back to London. Finally, we slipped them into the bottom of our cases, drowned them in clothes and tried hard to forget about them.

Six hours later, as we stood in the customs hall at Gatwick airport, June and I worked to appear relaxed. When the customs officer barked, "Anything to declare?" and stared at me, with a challenge written all over his face, I felt the sweat break out on the nape of my neck. "No sir," I lied, knowing that I was breaking the law. Pulling my suitcase towards him he smacked it flat on the table. As he ran his hands over the contents his eyes never left my face. He fiddled idly with the catches, as if teasing a threat. I tried to breathe and I tried not to whimper my fear. After a long moment, he waved a dismissive hand at both of us and said, "Go on."

June and I walked away as quickly as was decent, melting into the crowd.

Sanctuary

London
England
1963

In our evenings at squalid coffee bars and basement night clubs, we heard gossip about The Gateways, the one club all lesbians should join. The whisper was that it was in Chelsea, down the Kings Road, and on a side street. We were told it was almost hidden from view, and had an unimpressive green door with a small brass name plate. But finding it was only the first challenge. Getting in was the major obstacle. As a private membership club, one had to be invited as a guest by an established member. Finding the member was the real problem.

June was a social butterfly and could chat up almost anyone. But women would turn their heads and claim ignorance when she asked about the club. Finally, in frustration, we decided to just wander along the Kings Road, look out for women couples where one was dressed as a butch, and follow them.

Our first expedition brought success. We spotted a likely couple jump off a bus and walk along the street before turning a corner. Hurrying after them, we turned the corner just in time to see a green door close behind them. Nonchalantly, we strolled over and read the door plate: The Gateways. We'd found it! Now, to get in. We hung around asking several couples if they'd sign us in as guests, but the brusque "Not us" rejections were unanimous. After an hour we turned away, dispirited to be so near and yet so far!

Several weeks later, we mustered our courage and ventured back. We asked several couples to no avail, and then June asked a lone butch.

"Let's try," was her response, grinning at June. She rang the bell and we waited.

When the door opened, the woman filling the doorway was tall and muscular. She wore a man's suit with a thin string tie. Her dark hair was combed into a pronounced quiff, and she glared at our host. "Got two guests tonight," she said, causing the bouncer's eyes to cruise us up and down. Our Beatles suits and Chelsea boots did the trick, and she slowly opened the door.

We walked along a narrow corridor, towards a ground swell of juke box music and loud conversation. Cigarette smoke drifted up a steep flight of stairs.

As we worked our way down those stairs, we looked out over a room jammed with women dancing, drinking, talking and smoking. Many eyes swivelled to see who was entering and then glanced away. No one they knew!

My mind raced. We were in. This was the

height of London lesbian life.

At the foot of the stairs, at the reception desk, sat a strikingly beautiful woman dressed in a formal evening gown. Waving her cigarette holder at us, she asked our host, "How long have you known these two?"

"My guests? About ten minutes," she replied, as she laughed.

We were instructed to sign in and pay five shillings each, and told that any shouting or fighting would get us thrown out...for good. My hand shook as I signed and then laid out a ten shilling note to cover us both. We were directed to the cloakroom, where we hung our coats.

As we slid out into the main room and made our way across the crowded dance floor towards the bar, June's hand tugged on my belt. I turned and saw tears brimming in her eyes. Gently, I took her into my arms and we joined the other dancers. Throughout the evening she wept and laughed. How could she not? We were home.

Pervert

Welling, Kent
England
1963

My brother, Ian, had been married for several years when Jill, his wife, became pregnant. My parents were excited to be grandparents, and I wanted to share their joy. I was in my early twenties, enthralled by my life in the London lesbian scene where June and I were living in a social whirlwind of secret parties and bars.

I heard nothing from Ian and Jill directly: my mother kept me updated. Their son's birth was uneventful and they were grappling with young parenthood. And then one day Ian called and invited us for afternoon tea. This was big; we'd never been to their home. I'd always assumed my lesbianism made me persona non grata in their lives, although this had never been said. Now Aunty Gill was going to meet nephew Alistair!

It took us more than an hour and a half to travel from our flat in Central London to their small, brick-fronted, red roof tiled house in Welling, Kent. We chattered as we walked the half mile from the station, excited about this visit and hopeful that the gifts we brought were appropriate.

Ian and Jill received us warmly and served us square-cut sandwiches, sliced cake and scones. Clustered together in the living room, we nursed our cups of tea and chatted, as their quiet baby stared at us with big eyes. At six months, he was chubby, a real contrast to his tall, slender parents. The room was filled with baby gear; there was barely room for all of us. But the mood was light, and our gifts well received.

Around five o'clock Jill announced that it was time for Alastair's bath. She swept the baby into her arms and trotted off up the stairs. June and I helped Ian carry the dishes into the kitchen and started washing up. As we worked, Jill called down the stairs.

"June, want to come up and help give Alastair his bath?"

June and I tossed aside our tea towels and made for the door when Ian said,

"Not you, Gill."

June kept going as I stopped and turned to Ian, "What?"

Shrugging his shoulders, he said, "Well, you know."

"Know what?"

"Jill thinks you're perverted. It's better if you're not around kids."

I picked up the tea towel and kept drying dishes. Sounds of laughter floated down the stairs.

I was too stunned to speak. So I was the pervert, not June. Why me? Because I wore trousers and had a deep voice? And June was acceptable because she wore flouncy dresses with high heels? Whatever the reasoning, my own brother didn't intervene. I could share tea with him, but I was unfit to help bathe his son.

That was more than fifty years ago. I was never invited back. I do not know my nephew Alastair, nor his brother, Stephen. Today, if we passed on the street, we would be strangers.

Go Dance

Majorca
Spain
1964

In the spring of 1964, June and I joined tourists from Germany, France and Spain at Palma de Majorca airport, all of us bound for the same resort. Upon arrival, we crowded into the reception area where check-in was chaotic. Although we'd booked a room with a double bed, room assignments were now being made on the spot. The harried receptionist smiled weakly as she turned to us and said, "I know you girls won't mind a room with bunk beds—we don't have enough double beds and I have to give them to the couples." We minded a lot, but knew not to protest.

After a day of sunbathing, swimming and snorkelling, we dressed for dinner and dancing on the terrace. We'd chosen a table where we could see both the musicians and the water. We sat quietly, nursing our glasses of wine while we watched.

The young lads, gathered at one end of the bar, cast admiring glances when an attractive woman swung by. They didn't bother the couples, but June and I were fair game. Every night several of them would ask June to dance. She was attractive, with shoulder-length auburn hair and dark flashing eyes. Once on the floor, they were surprised by how well she danced—or rather, how she out-danced them.

I watched her in envy. I liked to dance, but the lads just knew not to ask me. I was dressed in white slacks and shirt, my short hair, my closed face, guarded.

We had not realised this would be such an isolated resort, miles from the nearest town, and with such limited options for the evening. I knew that June was dancing with the men to keep them at bay and to defuse the brewing frustrations they felt from being isolated, without girls in their midst.

By midweek, sitting by the dance floor after dinner had become too uncomfortable. Instead, we slipped away, changed into shorts and sandals, and went for a walk on the beach. That was where we could relax and chatter on, no longer on edge. But the following day, the young men found us on the beach and teased us, asking why we hadn't come dancing, suggesting we thought they weren't good enough for us. It was teasing, yes, but with a challenging edge. I laughed and June sparred back. We kept it light, but we knew it wasn't.

That evening, as we dressed for dinner, June told me, "You know, we have to go dancing tonight." When I asked why, her answer churned up all the fears and worries I'd dealt with since childhood. She told me that these young men were idiots, and it would take little provocation for them, as she said, "to rough you up." That was the price I would pay for being the one wearing the slacks. June was too femme; I was fair game.

I started to sweat. I was scared. This wasn't London. This was an isolated resort. I nodded. We had no option.

We settled at 'our' table and ordered drinks. The breeze was gentle and the air fresh. We made light conversation and watched folk dance. Occasionally, a lad came over and asked June to dance. An evening much like those earlier in the week. That is, until a voice at my elbow said, "Why don't you and your girlfriend dance? Go on," he added, gesturing toward the dance floor. I turned and gazed up at this wall of a man. He was over six feet, broad shouldered, clean shaven with massive forearms.

June laughed and I shook my head. "Maybe not a good idea."

He didn't move. He just stood there. "Why not?" he asked.

"Maybe the guys wouldn't like it," I replied.

He looked toward the bar. "Well then, I'll deal with them."

I looked at his calm face. My eyes asked if he thought this was safe and he nodded. I turned to June. She understood these blokes so much better than I did. When she smiled, stood, and held out her hand, I took it and led her onto the dance floor. We danced as the music moved from one song to another and a few couples smiled as they passed. Nobody said a word. Our new friend remained standing at our table, his arms folded as he watched us and the young men at the bar. When we returned to our table, he smiled and suggested we have a drink, assuring he'd check on us later.

At evening's end, he showed up as promised and insisted on seeing us safely to our room. Our last evening we took our table, ordered drinks and waited for the lads at the bar to make a move, but nothing happened. As soon as our "protector" arrived, we took to the floor with pleasure. We loved to dance. He stayed with us through the last dance and again walked us to our room. As I put the key in the lock, June thanked him and gave him a hug. He turned, shook my hand, and was gone.

Warning Bell

London
England
1965

Saturday evening at The Gateways became our special date night. Membership, which was a rite of passage, came with rules - no fighting, no drugs, no kissing in the bathrooms and no shouting. The dress code, if you were a butch, was slacks, shirt with cufflinks, tie, jacket, and dress shoes; short hair and no make-up. For the femmes, it was a dress or skirt with blouse or twin-set and stilettos. Also coifed hair, preferably a bouffant, and full make-up. There was to be no cross dressing, no changing gender-look from one week to the next. You picked your gender, dressed up and played the part. None of these rules troubled us as our roles regarding butch/femme were already well established.

When Saturdays rolled around, we arrived about seven-thirty. June settled in around a small table with a couple of friends, while we butches lined the bar getting the drinks. We were a noisy, boisterous bunch, and it was fun watching the mating rituals unfold. All of us revelled in our night out.

There were always women who arrived alone.

The butches headed for the slot machine or the juke box, or lounged at the bar. Playing the slots was an excellent cover for cruising the room, covertly eyeing up the femmes. The single femmes hung together in small gossipy groups, waiting to be chatted up or asked to dance.

Asking a lone femme to dance was easy: you asked her directly. Asking a femme in a couple was much riskier. First, you asked her butch partner if you could ask her girlfriend to dance. The butch would look you over and often refuse. If she approved, however, she'd look at her femme and nod. Then her femme was free to decide if she wanted to dance with you. If you made it to the dance floor, you knew the butch was tracking you closely. A crowded dance floor was preferable, because it allowed you to get away with a little hip bumping and grinding.

Everyone got to watch the humiliation if you were refused by either butch or femme. For a lone butch, there was nothing to do but retreat to the bar and sulk. A far more risky move was to ask a femme to dance while her butch was at the bar. Many a fist flew when the butch returned and found her femme dancing without permission.

Most of the time, I was successful when I made a dance request, mainly because I was out for the evening with June. And I knew better than to refuse butches who asked her, because she could take care of herself just fine!

Just before eleven the "last orders" bell rang and we began to gather ourselves to leave. Many of the older, smarter butches headed out with their girlfriends immediately. Only the diehards, the feisty "devil-may-care" butches were left. We all knew we faced the greatest risk.

A few miles away, at the football ground for Fulham, one of London's best loved football teams, home matches ended at five o'clock. Many a Saturday, hordes of young male fans streamed out of the grounds and into the pubs along the main road. As it happened, that road ran near The Gateways. These pubs rang their "last orders" bell at the same time, which meant that the streets were flooded with drunken fans looking for fun. We were the easy target.

The football bullies weren't interested in the femmes. Instead, they wanted to beat up on the butches and sought us out. If we, June and I, left as a couple, the louts would surround us, jostle and elbow us until we were separated and then rough me up. Punch, smack, low kicks: blows designed to shame, to hurt, to bloody, but not to kill. If we left in a bunch, with the femmes on the outside, we'd get name calling and harassment but no physical violence. But what real butch would hide behind her girlfriend? No amount of pleading or pressure from June to leave with others would change my mind. I was clear: we went in as a couple, we left as a couple.

Our plan rarely changed. Holding each other close, we would step out of the club and turn onto the street, fully expecting to be attacked. One week, three yobs surrounded us and I got a punch to my shoulder, a knee slammed into my thigh, and a hand slapped across the side of my face. I staggered, June pulled me upright, but I was immediately felled by a kick to my knee and then a blow into my back. My face hit a nearby wall, grazing the side of my cheek. Just as I prepared for another blow, a couple stepped out of the club and the yobs turned to their next target. June grabbed my arm, we ran around the corner and escaped...that time. Other Saturdays left me with a bloody nose and a black eye, but my pride was always intact.

Throughout these assaults, there was often a police car nearby, engine idling in case an emergency arose. The policemen watched this Saturday evening ritual. Never did one of them get out of that car.

Open Invitation

Orpington, Kent
England
1965

It was warm and welcoming in my mother's kitchen. The kettle gurgled when the water came to a boil. As the tea seeped, we worked in harmony, cutting sandwiches, laying out jam tarts and currant scones. Idle chatter about the garden and the weather flowed around us as we loaded the tea trolley. Preparing afternoon tea was a long honoured tradition for my mother and me.

But this time was different: I was jittery. A few days earlier I had gathered with friends to watch "Lesbians," an episode of Brian McGee's TV show *This Week*. The women interviewed appeared only in shadowed silhouette, fearful of losing their jobs or their families. For most of them, a life of hiding and lying was their only way of surviving. As I watched, I felt angry that most of the women were working women, not accomplished, professional women in the arts, science or business. But then I remembered that, in 1965, successful lesbians would lose their jobs if they spoke openly. As I watched the programme, I remember hoping that my parents weren't seeing this. And, if they were, that they wouldn't mention it. I really didn't want to discuss the show with them, nor my lesbianism.

I should have known better. As my mother bent to place a large plate of scones on the trolley, she asked if I'd seen the show. I struggled to keep my voice light, and then I lied, "No. What was it about?" I remember shuffling cups and saucers, fearful that my nervous, fluttery fingers would let them fall and break. She told me about the women they interviewed, most of whom were rejected by their parents and families and had lost career opportunities, "My only fear is that they may have lonely lives," she said. I heard her softly spoken words as an invitation. I mumbled something mundane as I turned away. At twenty-two I was still too scared to let her into my world. I had been hiding, passing, for so long that the expectation of rejection was my first response. No matter that I stood in front of her in my purple shirt, and my grey trousers, my hair slicked back and my heavy horn-rimmed glasses adding to my butch look. And no matter my parents always hugged and welcomed me and my girlfriends to their home, along with friends and family. Or that they never rejected me. I'd heard the women describe how their parents responded when confronted with their daughter's lesbianism, and I was afraid of that rejection from my own family.

With heavy shoulders and heart, I wheeled the

trolley into the living room. I knew my mother had been a brave woman to speak out. But it pained me deeply that I was not, and that I was the one who failed us both...miserably.

No Way Out

Eltham
England
1966

Life with June ended when I fell in love with Antonia. Together, we moved into my parents' house, into my childhood bedroom. This was a temporary measure, not very convenient, but a roof over our heads. Our privacy was limited because my mother still walked into our room without knocking. She reasoned we were all women, so why not?

Many evenings Antonia and I would climb into my little Austin van and drive into central London, where we spent time with our friends at a lesbian club. The van was our island of safety, hiding us from view—me in my standard butch outfit, and my femme Antonia, in a dress with high heels and a cape jacket. The van transported us from the privacy of our home to the exclusiveness of a members-only club, and it also represented our freedom to enter a world where we belonged.

Often, on the way home, we'd drive to the local lovers' lane. Secluded, with fields on either side, there were no lights and only minimal traffic. Settled in the van, we curled around each other, touching and kissing, with heavy condensation fogging the windows and rendering us invisible. Totally absorbed as we were, we were oblivious to the world outside.

On this particular night a sharp rat-a-tat landed on the driver's side window and startled us. We sprang apart, looking at each other in panic. I swore quietly as I grabbed my coat to hide my unbuttoned shirt and Antonia struggled to pull her dress down over her knees. At a second rap I wound down the window, only to be blinded by the strong glare from a torch. Peering up, I saw it was a man in uniform.

"So, what's going on in here?" he asked, his police helmet silhouetted against the late evening sky.

"Nothing." I stuttered, as I blinked in the light.

"Well, Sir," he said, and then suggested we were up to no good. He also pointed out that it was illegal to behave like this in public.

We sat still. My mind raced and I was so scared. I knew he could arrest me. I said nothing.

"Disturbing the peace is what you're doing. I can take you in for that."

I nodded mutely.

"So, Sir, where do you live?"

I told him.

"And you, Miss?"

"With him," Antonia replied.

"Oh, live together, do you?"

"Yes," I replied, "In my parents' house."

"So, why are you two doing this out here? Can't do this at home?"

I stared ahead silent.

He straightened up, slowly unbuttoned his jacket pocket and took out his notepad. As he flicked through for a new page, distorted voices and static from the CB unit fastened next to his collar punched through the still air.

"All right, what's your name?"

I took a deep breath and kept quiet.

"Come on. Know your own name, don't you?"

I nodded. "Gill Herbert."

He wrote it down and read it back. "Bill Herbert."

"No, Gill Herbert."

He bent down and looked in the window again. He stared at me. The moments hung long. And then he chuckled as he straightened up and put away his notepad. Placing both hands on the top of the door, he leant closer. "Well, isn't this a turn up? Got me a pair of lezzies!"

My stomach soured. I wanted to be sick.

"Well, here's what we can do," he said, as he chuckled some more. "I can take you both down to the station and book you for indecent exposure in public and for disturbing the peace..."

I waited.

"...or one of you, and I don't care which, can take a little walk with me behind that hedge and we'll have a little fun. Then we can all just forget about this."

Where was the choice? An arrest would be in the local paper, in a community where my father was the local headmaster. The scandal would stick. On the other hand, Antonia was only eighteen and mine to protect. I was older and should have known better. To add to the confusion, I was the only one who knew that I'd never had sex with a man.

He tapped his hands on the door frame. "So, what's it going to be?"

I saw no way out. I put my hand to the door handle. "Okay."

He stepped back. "Come on then."

I walked along the hedgerow and stepped through a gap, with him tromping behind. As we turned into the field he dropped his arm across my back and squeezed my shoulder. "Come on Gill, this'll be fun."

Antonia sobbed quietly as we drove home. My mother greeted us with hugs and told us our hot water bottles were already warming our beds. She asked if we wanted a warm night-time drink, but we declined. I started to shrug off my coat, but Antonia shook her head and I kept it on.

In our room, she gently reached for my coat;

I winced when I saw the grass stains on the back. When she pointed to my crotch, I saw a ragged, dark-brown blood stain on my trousers. For a moment we were still. We couldn't look at each other.

I grabbed my dressing gown, fled into the bathroom and filled the bathtub with scalding water. I sank into it, fighting not to cry as stinging pain shot through me. I tried to close my mind to the smell of crushed grass, the sound of the policeman's CB crackling in my ear, and the grunts and groans he muttered.

To this day I can still feel the roughness of his serge wool uniform rubbing my skin, and the ripping pain as he forced himself into me. Half a century later—these violent images still haunt me.

A Loud Voice

Beckenham
England
1968

Antonia and I moved to Beckenham, Kent, into a huge flat on the top floor of an old mansion. The building, subdivided into four units, with an outside staircase leading to our flat, had originally been a country manor house. Our home had four bedrooms, as well as a living room, dining room, kitchen and bathroom. Too big for just us, we often took in students as boarders.

I worked in the office of a local building contractor. Working with numbers was easy for me, so I enjoyed my role as company bookkeeper. Every morning I'd don a coloured blouse, along with a two-piece suit with skirt and jacket, slip on casual shoes, and walk into town to the office—maybe half a mile. The morning and evening walks cleared my head and allowed me to enjoy the neighbouring gardens, watching them change with the seasons.

One evening, as I strolled home, I crossed paths with the woman who lived in the flat below us. We paused, greeted each other briefly, and went on our way. Suddenly, she turned and asked if I knew the young man who lived upstairs from her. I shook my head slightly and looked inquiringly. She continued, "I just wondered," she continued, "because he and his wife row a lot and he has a really loud voice."

"No. Really?" I lied, then added, "Sorry, I've got to go," as I slid away. The brief encounter left me terrified. If she realised I was that young man, then she would know we were lesbians. And then she could rid herself of the loud young man by reporting us to the landlord who would evict us.

As I stumbled up the road, my heart racing and my mind swirling, I felt trapped and confused—suffocated. Yes, different clothes made me into a different person, with a distinctive stance and stride. And yes, I knew which clothes belonged to the actor and which to the authentic person. But what I didn't know was how to live with the dangerous fallout these multiple roles created. Nor how long I could live like this. What would I do when the price became too high?

Fair Game

Bromley
England
1971

I'd spent months pumping petrol in the pouring rain. This had been a great job for summertime but winter was a bitch. Cold feet and wet socks. I changed socks twice a shift, but my feet were never dry. Spare boots steamed in front of the two bar fire. They were warm to the touch, but cold and damp inside. I'd had to beg for this job, wanting desperately to be outdoors, wearing jeans and bovver boots, playing around cars, nobody critiquing me for my cropped hair or my bold stride.

Six months after I was hired, I found myself crying almost every day. The cold metal pumps stuck to my skin, ripping it off, and the steady rain dripped down my neck, soaking my clothing. The customers were curt, barely opening their windows against the merciless wind and then screaming at me as they squeezed credit cards or cash through the narrow slit. As for tips—a major part of my income—they dropped dramatically. I never understood why the worse the weather, the worse the tips. I expected them to be more grateful I was taking care of their cars, out there in the freezing cold, while they sat inside warm and dry.

But, much as I hated the weather, I couldn't quit. I'd not only resigned my position as a catering officer at the local college, but had abandoned the confining blouse and two-piece skirted suit in favour of jeans and shirts. I'd also abandoned all efforts to hide my butch self. By doing so I'd dashed my parents' dreams of a professional life for me. The price I paid to gain the freedom to be myself was very high, and there was no going back.

During this unsettled time, I'd tried to get a job as a ticket conductor on the London buses. They rejected me because I was too educated. When I protested that I really wanted the job, they explained it wasn't worth training well educated people because they didn't last. That was when I gave up and settled for pumping petrol.

So, I changed my wet boots for less wet boots and stamped back out through the puddles towards a large green van that had swung into pump number three. The driver, Mike, was a regular. From the warmth of his van he wound down the window and sang out "Fill her up, Gill." I splashed over and he smiled. "Not a good day for you," he said. "You're soaked." And then he climbed out of the van. I grinned and nodded. He was a nice guy; I didn't want to take out my frustration on him. As he followed me into the booth to sign for the petrol, he told me that he was looking for a good driver who could make deliveries. He was spending too much time on the road, and not enough time running the firm. I knew that I wasn't strong enough to deliver electrical contracting supplies, but I smiled and told him I'd think about it.

Two more days of sleet and ice saw me off the pumps and into the big green van. I liked the job. Every day when I got to work, the warehouse manager and the store men had already filled the van for my deliveries. Stan, the manager, handed me the route delivery sheet and off I went for the day. It was hard work, but there were always blokes at the jobs to help me unload. Away from the depot, I enjoyed listening to music, watching people and thinking my own thoughts, and I did it all while wearing jeans and boots.

On slow days, Stan asked me to help the store men sort and stack components in the warehouse. It was pretty mindless work and I was able to set my own pace.

It all worked well, except for Stan. It had taken him about two minutes to realise that I was a lesbian. And ten minutes to decide that meant I was easy prey. He would back me up into a quiet corner at the rear of the warehouse and grope me. No matter my protests, my pushing and wiggling to escape, he would bury his bristly moustache into my face with wet slobbering kisses. Chuckling, he would tell me that Stan the Man was going to show me what I was missing. Make a real woman out of me.

I knew Stan could fire me at the drop of a hat: the warehouse was his domain. Every morning, when I was handed my route sheet, I prayed the deliveries would take all day, and keep me away from him. I learnt the most circuitous driving routes and lied about traffic jams. When I had to work inside the warehouse, I listened for his footsteps and scrambled into areas with the other workers. I hung out in the ladies' room and the cafeteria, but I knew I couldn't hold him at bay forever. Scared as I was, I never mentioned it to Mike, afraid that he'd fire me for being a lesbian. I was trapped.

One day I couldn't avoid Stan. He tracked me down and swept me into his hairy arms. As he groped and kneaded, I knew his level of arousal was such that, this time, I wasn't going to be able to slide away. I became still: I waited. When I heard the zip on his fly, I took a deep breath, waited a moment, and then jerked my knee up with all my strength. He sagged back against the shelves cursing and swearing, grabbing his crotch. I ran. Out of the warehouse, across the street. Out of a job. I jumped into my car and shook all the way home. I cried most of the evening.

No job, no reference, no money. Back to square one.

Challenging a Cop

New Orleans
Louisiana, USA
1976

The door of the cafe flew open and in walked three cops. They swung their backsides up onto three stools at the counter. My lover, Patricia, and I sat in a large, comfortable booth eating breakfast. We had just arrived in New Orleans from Houston, Texas. As we ate, the cops ordered, then slurped coffee from oversized mugs and chatted with each other. All was calm. And then, slowly, one of the men—big and hulking—swung around on his stool, stared at me and frowned. I stared back.

"Excuse me, officer," said Patricia in her best Oklahoman drawl. "My friend just got here from England, and she's never seen a policeman in uniform, or your equipment up close." She smiled broadly as her foot came down hard on mine under the table. There was a moment of silence. No one moved.

Slowly the man's face changed. Grinning, he lumbered off his stool and came over to our booth. As he extended his hand, he said "Welcome to Louisiana," and slid into the booth next to Patricia.

Her foot continued to weigh heavily on mine.

I could barely breathe. I knew I had to shake his hand, so I did. Slowly and laboriously he removed every piece of equipment on his belt, including handcuffs and night stick, but he didn't touch his gun. As he laid them out on the table, he explained the function of each item. His voice carried clearly above the background noise of the café, but his words were lost to me over the radio crackling on his shoulder. I'd heard that crackle before. I knew men just like him. I nodded and smiled, but hated him. Finally his counter meal arrived and he left us. I looked down at my cold, unfinished food, my appetite gone. I felt Patricia's foot come off mine.

"Gillian, you have to learn not to look at cops," she whispered. "Just don't do it! They can feel your hatred. If you don't learn to hide, you'll get into big trouble."

She was right. I never learnt to hide.

Call to Action

Portland
Oregon, USA
2017

Many of my experiences occurred over fifty years ago, and in that span of time I have seen enormous changes in society's attitude towards gender issues. Like most people, I want to believe that we have all learnt to live with our differences. But the data says otherwise. In the US, in 2016, twenty-two transgendered people were murdered; the majority of them were women of colour. It is now September 2017, and twenty transgendered people have been murdered since the beginning of the year. Society's intolerance has shifted, found a new and vulnerable target. When will we learn to live with our differences, let alone embrace those who are different? It is my belief that telling our stories will effect change. Please, join me and tell yours.

Appreciation

My sincere appreciation goes to those who have worked diligently with me on honing my writing craft skills:

> Dimitri Keriotis
> Judith Barrington
> Sheila Bender
> Victoria Zackheim
> And the members of WOW writing group.

Others have stood with me and strengthened my resolve to write these gut wrenching tales:

> Patricia Barry
> Carol Biederman
> Julie Enszer
> Willa Schneberg

My deep gratitude to those who helped me heal:

> Dondi Kathman
> Edna Charrow
> Elaine Friedman
> Susan B. Day
> Dave & Sue Patch

Gillian

About the author

Born in Canada, raised in England, a California resident for thirty-five years, Gillian now lives with her spouse, Rita Silverberg, in Portland, Oregon. Her first memoir collection, "Spare Scenes" was published in 2012. Explore her work at www.gillianherbert.com

When not writing, she spends time in her glass studio creating fused glass bowls and platters.

www.ingramcontent.com/pod-product-compliance
Lightning Source LLC
Chambersburg PA
CBHW020658300426
44112CB00007B/435